T0132457

The Adventures of Texas Ruby

Jean Edwards

Copyright © 2023 by Jean Edwards. 848649

All rights reserved. No part of this book may be reproduced or transmitted in any form or by any means, electronic or mechanical, including photocopying, recording, or by any information storage and retrieval system, without permission in writing from the copyright owner.

To order additional copies of this book, contact:
Xlibris
844-714-8691
www.Xlibris.com
Orders@Xlibris.com

ISBN: Softcover   979-8-3694-1125-4
         Hardcover   979-8-3694-1126-1
         EBook   979-8-3694-1124-7

Print information available on the last page

Rev. date: 11/10/2023

Contents

Dedication

This book is dedicated to the children of our Military families, many of whom found a pet to ease the strain of deployment and transfers.

Texas Ruby Joins the Family

Sunlight glanced off the fuselage of the large silver plane as it sped down the runway until it gained altitude. On board, Master Chief Alvin Edwards contemplated the hardships his family would face without him in the coming year. He would be managing the hospital facility in wartime DaNang, Vietnam, so they would have to manage without him from 1970 to 1971. His wife, Jean, daughter Rose Anne (16 years old), son Larry (15 years old), daughter Jeanine (13 years old), and son Robert (only 8 years old). They had stood bravely in the terminal, and after saying their good-byes, he had left them by the large windows where they could watch the takeoff.

The sunlight gleamed off the wings of the plane as it flew higher and higher, until finally disappearing in the clouds. The family quietly went down the escalator and on to the parking lot.

The drive to their home in Rockville, Maryland was quiet. What was there to say? They were on their own as many military families before them had been.

They were stalwart in their resolve to make their father proud of their ability to manage their lives with the dignity he expected of them.

The house seemed quiet, and they endured a sense of change that permeated the house. They all quietly changed from their "send off clothes" to everyday attire. Nothing felt right but no one spoke.

To outsiders the family seemed calm and accepting of the situation, but each were sorting their feelings and doing their best to appear strong…except Robert, the youngest. He could not sleep at night. He worried that his father might be shot and dying in Vietnam.

Days passed and he still was unable to sleep because of war visions.

Finally, Jean decided to enlist help from a doctor. Her child's suffering was so intense he looked tired and ill from lack of sleep.

The Naval Base Doctor was very understanding. "Do you have pets, Mrs. Edwards?" he asked.

"Oh, no," she replied. "We have never had more than goldfish."

The Doctor thought for a moment, then took out a prescription pad, wrote a few lines, and handed it to Jean. The prescription read:

> Robert Edwards
> 1 Dog
> Signed: *Dr. Dailey*

"See that this prescription is filled," the doctor said.

Surprised, but willing to do anything to help her child, they returned home and called a friend who worked with the SPCA.

Mrs. Lundy knew of a litter of pups just down the street, and made an appointment for the family to visit.

The mother of the pups was registered "Princess Suzanne", the father, "O'Squeegy Beau". The seven Cairn pups were clinging to the mother with their teeth and were being carried about on her back.

"This is the puppy you can have. She is the runt of the litter, but would make a nice pet."

There was no way the lady could ever know the pup registered as "Texas Ruby" would bring happiness to a family struggling with worry and loneliness.

The Edwards family spent the next few days putting chicken wire on the wooden fence that surrounded their back yard, purchasing food, water dishes and a plastic clothes basket for a bed.

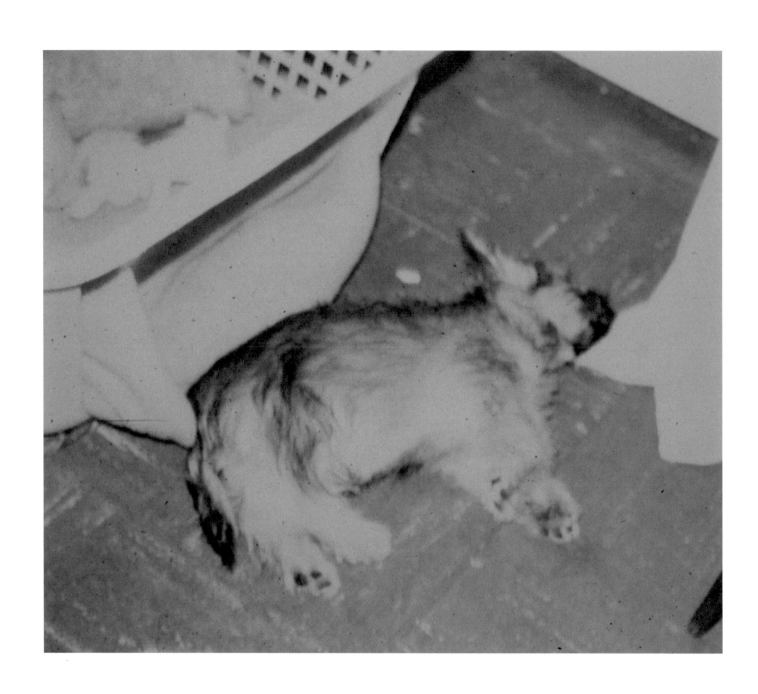

They cut a large round hole in the basket for an entrance, as Texas was much too small to jump over the rim. Next they found a soft furry stuffed dog for Texas to snuggle against if she missed her siblings.

A happy family was soon busy making sure little Texas Ruby was as happy as they, and everyone slept soundly that night.

Kitty-Dog

Time passed and the family settled down to life without the master of the house. Larry mowed the lawn, the girls helped with the housework and cooking. Texas learned to play "Kitty-dog", by batting a button swinging on a string wielded by one of the children.

The family decided that Texas should be cultivated and taught her to drink tea from a saucer at the table, which she took to immediately. After all, she was part of the family too.

When Larry called "Let's go watch the fishes," she ran for the stairs and watched the fish swimming about in the large fish tank in Larry's bedroom. The fish were colorful swimming about in their small manmade ocean where tiny porcelain bridges and castles had been placed among artificial sea ferns and rocks. Larry and Texas could be found, side by side on the bed, forearms stretched over the edge, watching the fish swimming about in their make-believe paradise.

Whatever they did, Texas joined them and wherever they went in the van, she had a front seat. Jean made her a black velvet harness with "Texas" embroidered in red on the band and red yarn tassels hanging on the sides.

Whenever she heard "Let's go for a walk", she would run to the place where it hung and wait for assistance.

When wearing her new harness she happily pranced on her walks knowing she was, indeed, a well-dressed companion.

Master Chief Comes Home

There was much excitement in the Edwards' household. The Master Chief had spent a year in Vietnam and in spite of some close calls, was coming home at last. The children had grown, and Texas Ruby had been added to the family.

The house had been cleaned, the woodwork painted and everyone bathed and put on their best Sunday clothes. Texas was bathed, her teeth brushed, and a ribbon bow was tied on her head between her ears.

The family arrived at the station in Silver Spring, Maryland, and the Master Chief arrived on time.

What a happy reunion it was! Master Chief slipped into the driver's seat of the van where Texas sat on the engine cover between the two front seats. Jean had taken the other front seat.

WELL!! It was clearly a change! Texas noted that no one seemed surprised that this "stranger" had taken over the driver's seat where Jean had always sat.

As the Chief backed the van out of the parking space Texas looked over at Jean. She didn't seem upset that this stranger had taken her place. Then she looked at Master Chief Edwards. Everyone was calm. Then she looked back at Jean…then straight ahead.

Things were certainly strange but Texas decided she would not complain if no one else did.

The family soon settled down as the changes in their lives became accepted. Robert learned to play

the piano and with urging, Texas would add her "oooo oooo ooooo" to the music. Texas remained on "guard duty" day and night. When a large tree in the back yard blew down with a thunderous boom, she hopped through the house on all four legs at once, while barking a warning to the family. She slept under the Chief's side of the bed at night, considering him the alpha dog. She had accepted him and adored him, cherishing any small attention he gave her. She never barked without reason, only as a warning if she thought there was danger. She always seemed to think needless barking by other dogs as ignorant.

Texas loved her baths and the brushing of her fur afterwards, and was meticulous with her food. At a BBQ a hot dog that fell in the dirt did not interest her, even when washed clean and cut in small pieces…she still turned her nose up as though it was inferior.

Her best guard duty was when Jean took an afternoon nap before going to officiate a gymnastics meet at a local college. Texas had been lying on the bed beside her when a noise woke them. Texas was off the bed and ran as fast as she could, barking angrily all the way to the front door where Mr. Bob, the mailman, had opened the door and thrown a package into the house, barely closing the door before Texas, with great fury, arrived.

Mr. Bob was astonished. Speaking through the screen door he said, "I can't believe Texas came after me!"

Jean explained that she was napping and Texas took guard duty quite seriously when she felt she was on watch.

Puddle Jumping

The family packed for the usual summer trip to visit family in Maine. They all crowded into the Dodge Lancer, Master Chief in the driver's seat, with the two boys beside him. Jean, Rose Anne and Jeanine sat in the back seat. Texas rode across the girls' laps and the family was soon on the way to visit grandparents and other relatives.

By the time they reached New York the skies had opened and it was raining in torrents. The August heat caused everyone to sweat and the gas tank was reading "empty" as they rolled past the state line.

Pulling into a way station for gasoline offered the opportunity to take advantage of the fast food and rest station.

Texas needed to "rest" also and there was nothing to do but let her out in the parking lot. When everyone returned to the car the last one in was Texas. Her abundant fur had absorbed water from the rain as well as from the puddle she had fallen into when she jumped from the car.

Taking her place in the laps of the girls in the back seat, their clothing was soaked and water streamed down their legs. They all wondered how one little dog could absorb so much water.

Invader

On a warm summer night Robert convinced his parents he should enjoy the adventure of camping all night in the backyard. He had explained that Texas would be with him in the tent "life guarding."

As the evening darkened the neighborhood grew quiet and boy and his dog settled down for the night in the tent that Robert's father had helped him set up.

Suddenly Texas charged from Robert's side and with barking and growling raised a great ruckus. Robert called for his father but by the time he vacated his bed and grabbed his flashlight, the clamor had ceased. Questioning the camping boy brought no answer as to why Texas had been so upset, so everyone returned to their sleeping quarters.

Ten or fifteen minutes later the clamor began again and everyone in the house responded to the ruckus.

Rob shouted, "Dad!! Texas has caught something!"

Sure enough, Texas had an opossum by the neck which she shook until it was rendered lifeless. The opossum had played "possum" one time too often and Texas had protected her family.

Texas Packs Herself

The family decided to vacation in Maine and unpacked for their stay in a small cabin by lake Passagassawaukeag. The following day they decided to go shopping in town.

Without much ado they prepared for the day. Robert arranged a soft bed from Jean's robe so Texas would be comfortable while the family was away.

When they returned Texas did not come running to greet them. They looked around and there seemed to be no sign of the little dog.

A suitcase had been left by the table and upon close observation one could see the cover was raised a couple of inches. A small black nose was seen at the opened edge. It was the nose of a small dog.

Texas had packed herself so she wouldn't be left behind when the family made the trip back home.

Big Dog – Little Dog

Whenever a disturbance erupted in the back yard Texas gave warning before attacking the problem. On a quiet summer day Robert called for his mother to come to the door because Texas had "caught something". Hurrying to the back door an amazing scene was being manifested.

Texas had indeed "caught" an invader, but it was not an opossum, it was a huge White Russian Wolfhound. It's back was nearly four feet high and it's proud head to an adult's shoulder. It had been shaved and groomed with long white fur pantaloons on it's tall legs.

One might say Texas, being 7 pounds of furred fury, had "caught" the intruder but it was fortunate the huge animal was a peaceful creature. It was pacing about the yard bewildered by the small dog who was hanging on it's neck by her teeth as the Wolfhound paced.

The family retrieved their "guard dog" and sent the Wolfhound on it's way.

Shore Leave

When Robert reached the age to be eligible to serve his country he decided to follow in his father's footsteps and join the Navy. After finishing training he attended Corps School and then was assigned as a Corpsman aboard the USS Detroit.

Following fire fighting drills he secured leave and blackened though he was he made the trip home for a short leave.

Texas was ecstatic over his return and Rob sat on one end of the living room couch while his Mother sat on the other end. Texas jumped up and leaned against Robert. Suddenly she looked up and glanced over at Jean. She realized that Jean's feelings might be hurt because she had chosen the homecoming Robert to sit with, so she quickly scrambled to sit beside Jean. After a few seconds she looked over to where Rob sat and with a look of concern - "scramble, scramble, scramble" back she went to be by Robert's side.

A few seconds later she looked over at Jean and "scramble, scramble, scramble" back she went to be close to Jean. To spare Texas' confused feelings of loyalty Jean went to the kitchen to prepare the evening meal so Texas wouldn't need to choose.

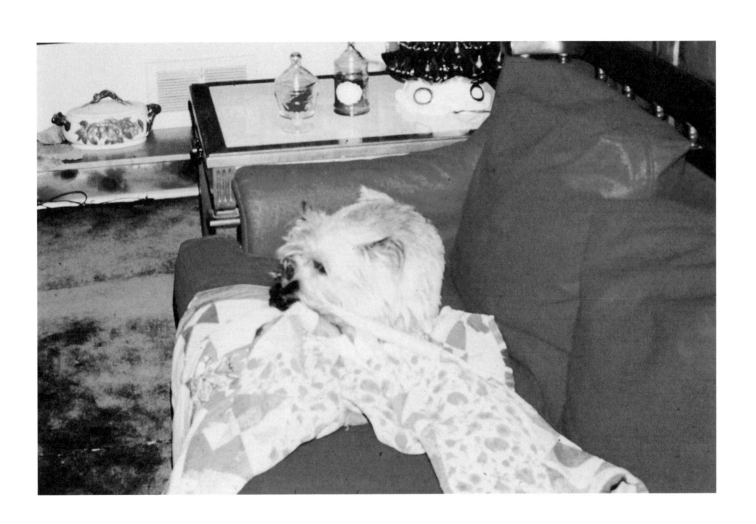

The Hospital

While the three older children were off to college, Rob was in the Mediterranean on a ship, Texas had only Chief Edwards and Jean at home.

Things went smoothly until Jean went to the hospital for surgery where she was a patient for a week. When she returned she lay on the living room couch to rest from the ride home.

Suddenly, out of nowhere Texas came running, jumped on Jean's feet, ran up her body and placed a paw on each side of Jean's cheeks…looking into her eyes with "Where have you been?" clearly expressed in her brown eyes.

Family

Time passed and the children had finished school, with Rose Anne teaching elementary school in West Virginia, Larry working at travel and vehicle design in the U.S Government, Jeanine had become a Program Director for the YMCA after a successful career of competition in gymnastics, and Robert having been selected for a commission in the Public Health Service upon graduation from college. Texas had grown older but still took her duty as family protector seriously.

Whenever the family gathered there was much reminiscing, with stories of Texas in the forefront. Her attitude concerning her duties as watch dog had always been a source of amusement as she was absolutely dedicated to being the family protector…except when the Chief was home. When he walked through the door after his day of work at the National Naval Medical Center she would lie down with a "now it's your turn" look. The family was always amused by her attitude. Texas worshipped the Chief and slept under his side of the bed at night, secure in her belief that protecting the family was Alvin's job when he was home.

When Christmas came, Texas had learned to open packages and after she opened her own she helped Robert open his, then danced on her hind legs in appreciation of the occasion.

She delighted in her walks, wearing her black velvet harness with the red tassels, prancing happily with the knowledge she was a well dressed canine.

Perhaps she was spoiled, but the family was happy with her dainty manner, knowing she would immediately change her attitude and become their protector if she sensed danger.

The family decide to take a break from work, and visit Rose Anne in West Virginia.

The Last Act of Valor

Robert returned home following his duty on the Detroit, and prepared for his career with Public Health Service. The family was gathering in West Virginia where Rose Anne lived in an apartment.

Since graduating from college she had taken a teaching job in West Virginia. Robert joined her and her friends in the pool at her housing complex. There was much happy shouting and splashing easily heard from inside the apartment where the Chief, Jean and Texas were resting after the long drive to West Virginia.

Texas became alert when she heard the shouting and although she was old and frail she bounded through the open door. Having recognized Robert's voice in the shouting she mistakenly thought he was in trouble, crying as she ran, she jumped into the pool and swam to her beloved master to save him.

There were many tears shed as the brave little dog was wrapped in a towel in her Master's arms. Robert carried her back to the apartment where she was towel dried and received much tender petting in appreciation of her bravery.

Printed in the United States
by Baker & Taylor Publisher Services